Praise for Michael Flanagan:

"Michael Flanagan is a master story teller, using the poem to drive it all home with economy of words, the might of a sawed-off shotgun, and genuine compassion. You get more out of a 30 line Flanagan poem that you will ever get out of most novels. While the nature of his poems are often dark, with tales of drugs, death, suicide, and other terminal events, Michael treats his subjects with kindness and humanity without pulling any punches. He is a *Nerve Cowboy* chapbook contest winner, a long-time favorite at the magazine, and an exceptional poet in a time when we need them the most."

-Joseph Shields
Editor of *Nerve Cowboy Magazine*

There are a lot of wounds in poetry. It can be a much rarer thing for those wounds to strike with deep honesty. In Michael Flanagan's new collection, *Days Like These*, broken truths ride on a hard straight language, the kind of writing that makes the reader see their own lives, and become enveloped by the strange trick of warmth that resides in heartache. Family. Friendship. Childhood horrors. Death. Addiction. Searching always for meaning, Flanagan's work delves into the ugliness of everyday life, the poems enough to shake you to tears in all the right ways.

-Ted Jonathan, Author of the poetry collections, *Bones and Jokes*, and *Run*

Days Like These

Poems by Michael Flanagan

Luchador Press
Big Tuna, TX

Copyright ©Michael Flanagan, 2019
First Edition1 3 5 7 9 10 8 6 4 2
ISBN: 978-1-950380-70-1
LCCN: 2019954163

Design, edits and layout: El Dopa
Cover and title page image: Jon Lee Grafton
Author photo: One Eyed Jack
All rights reserved. No part of this publication may be reproduced or transmitted in any form or by any means, electronic or mechanical, including photocopying, recording or by info retrieval system, without prior written permission from the author.

Acknowledgments:

Some of these poems previously appeared in the following publications:

American Dissident; Barbaric Yawp; Chiron Review; The Examined Life; Mad Poet's Review; Main Street Rag; Mas Tequila Review; Misfit Magazine; Naked Knuckle; Nerve Cowboy; Paterson Literary Review; Presa Press; Quercus Review; Slipstream Magazine; Streetlight Press; Subprimal Poetry Review; Trailer Park Quarterly; Trajectory; Tribeca Poetry Review; Zygote In My Coffee and the chapbook, A Million Years Gone, from Nerve Cowboy's Liquid Paper Press

Thank you to Tony Gloeggler and the man from the Bronx, for being first readers par excellence. And a very special thanks to Rebecca Schumejda for getting my foot in the door.

TABLE OF CONTENTS

Twenty Years / 1

To Think She Broke My Heart In 1983 / 3

Life, You Know / 5

Oblivious / 7

Some of Us / 8

Ben Webster's Saxophone / 10

Eldon / 11

Happy / 13

Before His Sixteenth Birthday / 15

Cathy / 17

A Night Like This / 19

The Knights of Columbus on 30th St. / 21

Besotted / 23

Holy Grail / 25

Dying / 26

Mourning / 28

Before Things Took A Turn / 30

1986 / 32

Train Wreck / 34

awake you want to start a dream but / 36

Watercolors / 37

The Making of a Writer / 39

Speaking of Art / 40

Angie / 42

Earth / 44

No.3 School / 46

Big John / 47

Broken / 48

When We Were Young / 50

Crossroads / 51

Gone / 53

Brother / 54

Shadows / 57

Dale / 59

Story / 62

You Turn Eighteen (Tucker Pavilion Adolescent
   Psychiatric Ward) / 63

The Sound A Rattlesnake Makes / 65

child / 66

Today / 67

Funeral / 68

Replenishment / 72

A Simple Thing / 73

Everything / 75

About Fourteen Years Old / 76

Trick or Treat / 77

Poem Written Upon My Daughters Graduation
   From Elementary School / 79

It Wasn't An Unusual Night / 80

Crazy / 82

Mental / 84

Support Specialist For Mentally
   Challenged Adults / 86

Nothing / 88

911 / 90

Falling / 92

August / 94

Listen / 96

Other World / 97

Eying The Clock / 99

Taboo / 102

Danny / 104

Danny, Again / 106

Locked Unit Psych Ward Cornel Medical Center
   New York City / 108

Mea Culpa Mea Maxima Culpa / 111

The Alarm Rings / 112

Words / 114

For Darcy; not only my daughter,
but my very good friend.

Twenty Years

The place was in Manhattan, one
hundred and ten dollars, twenty-five
years ago. We were both nineteen. We
said we loved one another. We went
up in a small green elevator, got off
on the 4th floor. The receptionist asked
for the money and I paid her. About
twenty minutes later they called her in.
When it was over, we concentrated
on small talk. Three weeks after that,
in an Irish pub on 8th Ave., drunk
on beer, she screamed, You have
no fucking idea what I went thru, there
were hoses, she said, and lights so
bright they were like spot lights. She
ran back toward the bathrooms, tears
streaming out of her eyes. It's been
at least twenty years since I've seen
her, and it still doesn't matter that
I'd wanted to grab her that day
in the waiting room, tell her,
to hell with this, take her back
down in that elevator, make her
understand her father wasn't going
to kill her, that, god dammit, I had
a job, we could get a place of our

own, she could finish school,
that we'd only said the word
pregnant once, and never said
the word baby at all.

To Think She Broke My Heart In 1983

A cop out of his cruiser tapped the window
with a clacking of something metal on glass.
Pressed against one another in the front seat
of the '76 Le Sabre we woke confused, as if
we'd known things bright and sure before
but had been drained of all of it during our
illicit rest. Seventeen years old, parked in each
others arms at the end of another ping pong
night of booze and half wit gatherings,
empty conversations. The pre-dawn light
was as much of a surprise as the badge,
the gun, the inquiry into our state of being.
The law didn't care about much other than
whether we were victims in blood of some
late night crime. Dumb as any other kid
on the edge of growing up I felt like a man
when he adjusted his sidearm and said he
guessed I'd want to get the lady home before
her people grew too worried. What I wanted
was to share nights and days, bills and children
with this girl. It was love and it was every-
thing, as it always manages to be when you
know nothing about it. This hard headed girl,
volatile, possessed of cruel humor, sulking
when anything didn't go her way, I would

have married her any day of the week, spent
Sunday's at the bar watching the game, Friday's
after work drinking with the guys. Three kids
eventually. Meals once a week at grandma's.
One trip to Disneyland before the children
weren't young anymore. Mortgage, lawn care,
car payments. I'd have joined the Elks Club
or the Knights of Columbus. Easter egg hunts.
Church Sunday morning. We'd have celebrated
the Fourth of July, said we loved one another
and almost believed it, a random first love
stretched thirty years. Neighbors helping install
the above ground pool. One vacation in Europe
that never happens. A lake house somewhere
you started wishing you could afford. Young
in our parents way, old like them. Death almost
a blessing when it finally grows near, trying
to congratulate ourselves on just getting through.

Life, You Know

I see this photo all the time
and don't much give it a
second thought, but then
once in a while it stops me,
I reach over and pick it up,
it's my daughter when she
was five years old, standing
near the railing of a boat, the
statue of liberty in the back-
ground, some family outing
we were on but that's not the
thing of it, this look she has,
the smile and her shoulders
pulled up a little bit, it's pure
innocence, joy and simplicity,
it breaks my heart, she's nine
now and still soft, still open,
she loves and she feels and
she holds things dear, she
has small adventures with her
friends and still loves to tell us
about them, but I think, what
will come? six years, eight
years, fifteen years from now,
this beauty, this purity, it can't

last, things will break and they
will be glued back together and
they'll break again, a light will
dim, it might even go out, bits
of hard road will accumulate,
life, you know, no one escapes
it, and all I can think, holding
that picture, moving it closer
and closer to see every bit of it,
is i'm going to have to watch,
and there'll be some things,
but really very little, I can do
to make any part of it better

Oblivious

In her business suit, in a bar
down near Wall St., about eight
o'clock on a Wednesday night,
bartender hands her the phone,
she talks into the receiver,
obviously speaking to a child:
*Honey, I am coming home. Yes.
Soon. Yes honey, I promise.*
She hands the receiver back
to the bartender. As he takes
it, she rolls her eyes, as if
acknowledging they are
comrades, two people who
understand the fight, how
hard it is when others want
something different than
your cause. Smiling now,
she shakes the tumbler in
her hand and orders another
drink, oblivious once again
to all but the ice cubes
at the bottom of her glass

Some of Us

There were fences and garage roofs and alleyways with hidden fire escapes, but best was the bay at the edge of the city, polluted by oils and waste from the Newark refineries, dirt for a shore, rocks and deep giant holes dug by delinquents, the holes covered over with sheets of splintered plywood, we used to hide in there, smoke cigarettes, light things on fire, dirty rags, weeds, old dry pieces of driftwood until our clothing and hair reeked of smoke, we practiced cursing and spitting and drinking, men on the bum would traipse around there collecting bottles, drinking wine, we watched them carefully, threw rocks at them sometimes and ran away, one was a woman we called seahag, we'd follow her, call after her until she'd turn and scream, we never made it home for dinner on time, fall or summer we ran wild, the water and the filth and the rats and old tires, no one bothered us down there, other kids rode their bikes, played ball, collected baseball cards but we travelled the odder corners and felt at home, later some of us became drug addicts, some became nothing, we were all scarred, our beginnings damaged one way or another, none of us went to school much or did anything when we were there, we had problems at home too, and some of us found barstools, some died early, some receive disability checks every month, gone in the

head, some of us have children who are not on the
straight and narrow, who have troubles at home
and in school, I think one of us became a cop, one
ran away and joined the army, another writes poems
and another is a garbage man, it was all a long time
ago, and some of us remember and some of us don't

Ben Webster's Saxophone

The last three days it has rained like monsoon season here.
Watching everything darken you ended up counting people
you'd grown up with who had died young: Tommy Kelly,
Angelo Santiago, Cathy Lucas, Bobby Lucas, Billy Cody,
Billy's younger brother, who's name you can't remember,
Mark Caramanno, Robert Murphy, Kevin Klich. All gone
before the age of twenty-five. All from drugs, or suicide,
except Bobby Lucas, who was playing around with
a handgun when his best friend, pointing it at Bobby's
head, accidentally let the trigger slide back. You don't
know if that friend is alive or dead, what kind of life
he's lead. Sufficient to say his nickname was Pills.
You do like rain though, the scent before and after
it comes, the way it shakes things, the sound
of it through trees, on asphalt, as car tires roll by.
Why are poems so often death and sadness, the past
like a creep on your lawn, staring in the window.
It's Ben Webster's saxophone now, as you take a break
from writing and wait for the kettle to boil. Those
notes, low in the register, elongated, they never spell
out meaning, though they never make you laugh,
always heart wrenching. Tears and remorse.
We crave them more than apple pie.

Eldon

Eldon wakes at two a.m., goes to bed at six in the evening, arrives at the center by eight in the morning and never stops moving the entire time he's there. Forty years old he looks twenty-five. Walks like Chaplin's tramp, if the tramp had a bent spine and supports around his ankles. The man curses like a glass blower when the heat shatters his globe, yells and cries and grabs staff in crab like claw grips when loud noises make anxiety overtake him. *No more of that,* he'll say when one of his fits are done. Mostly he tries to work, cleans bathrooms, fill the vans with oil, write reports, none of which he can accomplish in any way, but bless him, he wants to. Leaving a room he'll wave a crooked finger. In his high pitched voice he'll say, *Michael. Michael. Watch the phone. Back in a minute.* He claims he needs to change Marissa. Eldon loves Marissa. Marissa appears not to know anyone exists. Day after day she moans, walks around manipulating a small yellow shovel, the plastic kind that comes with kid's beach pails. She screams too, apparently for no reason at all: change her diaper, feed her, comb her hair, hope that like an infant she settles down. Eldon says, *Hey Marissa, can I ask you a question?* She keeps right on walking, glazed eyes, drool on her chin. It's me that drives Eldon home at the end of the day. He talks the whole way, turns dials on the dashboard, presses the button that pops the trunk, slides the seat back, puts his feet up on the dash.

"Look Michael look." "I see Eldon." "Who did it Mike? Who broke the chair?" "You did Eldon. Now stop hitting my buttons or you'll have to sit in the back." He laughs, pushes them again, tells me he loves me if I get pissed. When he sees a cop chasing a speeder he goes wild, yelling, *Goddamn Mike. Ah shit. Pull over.* He tells me, *Fuck you,* when I insist they're not after us. I think he longs to be hunted by the authorities, to go on the run after some misdeed, a bank robbery or kidnapping, wants the world as awake as he is, lights flashing, guns drawn. Eldon lives with his mother and sister. They dress him in Old Navy, matching socks, underwear. His Fred Flintstone lunchbox has a multitude of snacks, fine dressed sandwiches, cross cut with the crust gone. He insists he's going to move out. I tell him he's got it made, to stay where he is, as if there's a real option. *Call you Mike,* he says. *"Get an apartment." "Who Eldon?" "Me."* Monday's he claims he went on a date on the weekend. *"Who did you take Eldon?" "Vanna White."* He wants to drive, pull into a gas station, get gas, go to the grocery store, to the Verizon Phone Center. He'd love most of all to do these things on his own, but he's never even been to the mailbox without supervision, and he never will

Happy

I lie down. I stare at the wall, wondering who in this world
is happy. I've heard Jack Nicholson is. George Burns, maybe
Sophie Tucker when they were alive. They must have found
the loophole I've been looking for. Last week, in the Styles
section, the Sunday Times reported the Bowery has been
completely renovated. Suites in boutique hotels near Houston
and Bowery are running 3,000 a night. Suede is popular
around the doorways men used to sleep ugly dreams off in.
My poems and stories pile high, published in places
almost no one reads. The August heat is out in force today.
A brief rain and there's steam off the road. Still I feel a chill,
like some bogeyman hidden in the trees has turned
the world into a cold cellar. Dollars to donuts gamblers
continue to cross the street when they pass a cemetery.
Help me Rhonda, help, help me Rhonda. Well, there was
this birthday party last week. It was for a client, a guy
who goes to the center for mentally challenged adults,
where I earn my living. The party was at a bowling alley,
dimly lit, tragic smelling. His sister ran the celebration,
loud mouthed, half drunk. Her husband sported
all the accoutrements, towel to wipe the ball,
powder and the wrist thing they wear for God knows
what reason. The man kicked a leg out behind him,
bowled frame after frame. My man Eden, the birthday boy,
also has Cerebral Palsy. What in the world (ask the sister's
husband I'd guess) was anyone thinking, holding this thing

at a bowling place. Four people besides family members
showed up. None of them were friends of Eden's,
who is verbally hard to understand, and can't function
without minders. Thankfully they set up a stand for him,
a contraption built of aluminum. It slanted down on a curve.
You were able to place a ball on top and a person could
come up and push it off. Every time Eden used it, after
the ball started down the lane, before it got near the pins,
he'd turn and look at the crowd behind him. With this giant
grin he'd say, look everyone, look. I think I was the only
one that did. I can tell you, it was beautiful.

Before His Sixteenth Birthday

He's a kid, I guess about fourteen.
The high school's up the block and
he's coming from there. As we pass
each other I see his face has been
marked with a pen, lines on his
nose, at his eyes and mouth, long
lines making an odd design like
a mask. The pen is in his hand. I
guess he wants to make sure I
see all this because he raises the
hand with the pen and waves at
me as he goes, looking kind of
angry, as if all the trouble he's
ever seen in his life has been
my fault. Poor kid, I think,
those are tough years he's in,
he obviously has a wacky
way of dealing with it which
probably doesn't go over too
big in the old school yard.
He'll probably make a fine
writer someday, maybe a
painter if he knows how to
hold the brush and work the
colors, if he doesn't end up

in the basement first, a rope
tied around a pipe, noose
slipped over his head,
kicking a box of christ-
mas decorations out from
under his feet, tears like
old rain in a gutter smudging
his face, feeling more alone
than he believes anyone else
ever has, a month or so be-
fore his sixteenth birthday

Cathy

Later she'd have two kids, a husband in the Marines, almost a calm life before she went up the walkway onto the bridge, flew into the air and lived, only to find the same railing a year to the day later, step over it and die. But this was a softer night, years before. You were a teenager, alone in your room. Dylan's Blood On the Tracks probably played on the turntable, the songs like mazes, the endless stories until you rose and stretched, feeling the absence of almost everything wrapped around you as you walked down the stairs, out the door. The block then, full of cracked brownstones piled on top of one another, the way anyone walking by could hear arguments through open windows summer nights, families gathered at their dinner tables. She was on her stoop, blonde in a tank top, pair of cut off jeans, no shoes or bra. When you were eight or nine, you'd watched police and rescue workers take her father away, the only person you'd ever seen, outside of cartoons, strapped into a straight jacket. It was after that she'd started playing that game, her and a friend, on their bikes, in the street, coming as close to passing cars as they could, getting knocked down sometimes, taken away in an ambulance. Her brother too, at nineteen, accidentally shot in the face by his

best friend, playing with a gun, blown away.
So many years you'd known her and hardly ever
spoken to her. That night though you both said hello.
You sat next to her when the Mad Russian came
out on his roof. Drunk again on beer, he lashed out
at the neighborhood, one accusation fired toward
each family, starting at the north end of the block,
working his way down. At Cathy's house he went
silent. Then he called your name: Flanagan. Who do
you think you are? Shanty Irish, I see you there.
People looking from their windows, shaking their
heads, smiling. Her eyes, in the dim street light,
a clean blue, almost water. A small bottle of wine
by her leg, the two of you passing it back and forth.
Her crying once, not saying why. Tears stopping, she
leaned over and kissed you. Getting up before you
could say anything, she ran inside. You waited
a long time, but she never came back out.

A Night Like This

Tonight the eyes don't care and the
head is a monument to fog, too
tired even to stand and look out a
window, too tired to drive to the
liquor store or love a beauty queen,
if there happened to be a beauty
queen available to love, a train,
that's what would be right on a
night like this, an empty platform,
a sharp chill in the air, the hours
sweet darkness and abandon,
some kind of sadness and
longing and trouble, a light,
dim and yellow at the far end of
the station, you wait and wait and
finally the tracks rattle, rolling
metal on metal, closer and closer,
it pulls in, two or three passenger's
scattered here and there, hardly any-
one at all, the conductor, bored or
half drunk, nods at you, finding a
seat you sink down then prop
yourself up again, you press your
forehead against the window,
you watch the spot where you
were standing a minute ago,

the world seems empty of any-
thing but strangers, the train
moves and things start to
go faster, and you know you
won't sleep until you are there

The Knights of Columbus On 30th St.

My father was a member of the Knights of Columbus, held office there and had keys to many doors including the banquet hall on the third floor. They had dances on the third floor weekend nights and Sunday afternoon I would steal the keys and my friend and I would sneak up to the hall and run around, yell loud whoops for the large echo the emptiness gave, do all kinds of nonsense but mostly we were there to drain the left over beer at the bottom of the kegs behind the bar. We would fill a pitcher each and gulp thru the foam. We were eleven and twelve years old and drank quickly to prove we were men and we got drunk fast. Middle of one Sunday afternoon we split seven pitchers of that warm foamy beer, staggered back down the stairs, out the door and down the block. We were beery and boisterous and I remember we sat on the lawn in front of my house yelling at whoever passed by, anything that came into our heads, not a care in the world. Friday and Saturday nights belonged to the women in their gowns, the men in their suits, they danced together, drank, ate, applauded the band. The Knights of Columbus on 30th St., sometimes it seemed like my father lived there. He liked rye and water, beer or vodka martinis. Many days and nights he staggered home, an angry drunk mad at nothing, at everything, mostly at us, ugly words on ugly nights. My father, a drinker who when he drank drank until it was gone. At home on a barstool, best at tipping the barkeep, ordering a round, singing, stomping. I hated him for it. He was a sloppy drunk and I wanted to blow the Knights of Columbus building up, as if it harbored the only bar in town, as if everything would be better once it was gone

Besotted

My mother stayed with my father thirty years. His social life
was the corner bar. She got together every Wednesday and went
to the movies with other neighborhood wives. I never saw my
parents hug, or dance, never saw them share a joke together
or linger over cups of coffee. All his faults seemed to go with
him into the grave, my mother more in love with my father
after he died. Tell me, if your spouse left you how would it feel
knowing you could open any window, make the bed or leave it,
drink gin in the morning, stare at another's body without
repercussions. I haven't said a word to my wife in ten years
that hasn't seemed redundant. Two decades after my father's
heart failed the final time, my mother has gone. At her wake
three childhood friends come in. Talking to them I remember
the sound of spaldeen balls bouncing off schoolyard walls,
the small torture of trying to win games against one another.
In our teens we drank together, lied about girls, fell in and out
of love, graduated high school, drifted apart. Nostalgia swells
the funeral parlor air as the bald one with glasses, Gregory,
kind even in his youth, says we have to get together more often,
twenty-five years is too long. We four smile in agreement,
none of us probably believing it will happen. Days later,
home in the usual chair, I stare at the television, lost in a scene
from a halfwit episode of some comedy drama I've watched
too many times before. On the floor beside me there's a dream,
an attic garrett full of paint brushes, canvasses, a room above a bar

in Prague, or Amsterdam, Paris, Guam. Besotted by nacho chips and pizza, I listen to my seventeen year old daughter come in the front door. The light on the tv screen blinks and I think, no wonder her and her friends seek the odd comfort fog of weed, no wonder songs of broken love and rusted things seem far more real. On the phone later my brother tells me we've moved up on the shelf, orphans in the world, we're now next in line for the eternal beyond

Holy Grail

There's nothing like a puddle when you're a child.
There's nothing like a drink when you're twenty.
There's nothing like death when you're fifty, a thing
far away and closer than anything. People talk about
the same ball teams they fought over when they were
twelve, listen to the same music, nothing but what
they first heard forty years ago. Each of us seems
to be on our own train tracks, riding the engine
that will derail someday. Drunk at fifty is depressing.
Everyone eventually stops jumping in puddles. Still
I remember the corny tune I asked the dj to play
at prom because it was love and would be forever.
I haven't seen that girl in thirty years. If I'd been
a minute older, an inch less shy, there wouldn't
have even been a first date with her. Insecurity
drives you into odd places. Believing everyone's
better at life can make a person take what they
can get, accept it as the holy grail. The lesson
of age remains what might have been. As long
as there's time there's hope. Forward. Backward.
Standing still. The worst that will be found
is the very end of the cliff.

Dying

You walk toward the eastside, along the
park, smoking angel dust. Near the Plaza
Hotel, the drug convinces you everyone
watching you believes you are famous.
In front of the Plaza's fountain you sit
in a fog of imagined accolades. When
you buy a pepsi in a deli, you remember
you used to work over on 55th St. You
go there, look at the building, wonder
what year it was the last time you went
thru those doors. It was your father who
got you your first real job, on Maiden
Lane, close to Wall St. You were eighteen,
intimidated by the plushness of the offices,
the suits, ties, the grown women in business
attire. You can still hear the sound of his
voice the day he called wanting to meet
you for a drink after work, how you claimed
you had to work late because his drinking
embarrassed you and you didn't want to be
with him, the disappointment you felt in
yourself later that night, learning he'd lost
his job after twenty-five years. Rolling
another joint, you think about when you
used to walk from this building to the

subway practicing different speeches you
might give if you ever became an actor and
won an Academy Award. On 8th Ave., you
watch the tourists lined up in front of the
small depot on 54 th St., waiting for an empty
tour bus to arrive. You use the bathroom
in the McDonald's on the corner, then start
back toward Central Park, thinking of
your dad now, slowly dying in a hospital
bed in the living room of your parent's
New Jersey home, how badly you want
to be clear headed, straight, when the
call finally comes saying he's gone

Mourning

I knew a man who loved art and
had his pencils and charcoals as a
boy, then for fifty years he sketched
nothing, painted nothing. When he
was sixty-three and retired he built
a studio in the basement of his home
and went back at it, but it was too
late, two years later he was dead.
At the end he'd thought he was just
getting started, he was at a point
where he thought he was warming
up to it, that he was beginning to
learn a bit, then he was gone. There
are rumors, but I don't think we
come back. There are rumors, but
I don't think we get heaven. He
spent his working life in an
office, writing numbers into
account ledgers. I guess I knew
him as well as anyone can know
another person, I was his son,
and I can tell you, until that base-
ment he never talked about art or
read books about art or knew the
lives of any artists. He never went

to museums to see Picasso's or Van Goh's or de Kooning's, and now he's dead, and his story can't change, it won't have any other kind of ending, ever.

Before Things Took A Turn

Thru Central Park, down beautiful
5th Ave., warm spring day, people
teeming by. On broadway and 47th,
in a tunnel of your own mind, you
imagine tourists mistaking you
for a famous star. In the Village,
in Washington Sq. Park, you stand
for 3 hours without moving, you
think of yourself as the freest
being on earth. On a wall, outside
N.Y.U., you fantasize about coeds,
think about higher learning. Near
3rd St. and Thompson, you see
an announcement in the window
of the latest incarnation of Gerde's
Folk City: Ginsberg will be per-
forming that night, a reading
backed by music. In honor of
Howl, you swallow 3 more hits
of mescaline. Later, watching the
show, you concentrate on beards,
on moccasins, you hardly hear a
word spoken. Past midnight, you
walk the 40 blocks to Times Square,
watch the freaks there watching

you, your eyes blown wide open,
sparks shooting from them like
rounds from an m16, streams of
light obliterating the dark horizon

1986

The room key came attached to a long fat
piece of wood, the room number in spray
paint down the center of it. The hotel was
on 49th and 9th Ave. It was dim and ugly,
holes burnt in the carpet, in the bedspread,
a sour odor in the hallway, the smell of
urine in the elevator. Oddly, the room
didn't have a telephone. You were lucky
though, there was a small television on
the bureau. You snorted a bag of heroin,
did a few lines of coke, stared at Jimmy
Stewart, in a western, on the Turner
Broadcast Network. Later you listened
to the noises thru the walls, muffled
voices, pans or some similar thing
rattling when they were dropped.
Eventually, people began to fuck in
the next room, you heard the bed
squeaking, the grunting. You realized
then this was just the way a person
like you might go out, dead of an
overdose at 4 am, the lights of an
ambulance burning red and blue in
the filthy snow by the curb. The whole
night you sat on the edge of the bed,

fixed there as if you were afraid the
rest of the room was contaminated.
Six in the morning, high and paranoid,
You went down to the front desk and
checked out. You remembered then
what day it was, thought, probably not,
but maybe if you'd looked out your
window you'd have seen the ball drop,
Dick Clarke on the roof in Times Square,
his black leather gloves, his camel hair
overcoat, the noise and confetti, the
cops on horseback, keeping order

Train Wreck

This guy, we called him Jack the whack,
philosophy professor out of Arizona, heroin
addict, used to try and slow that train wreck
down by wrapping his dope up neat and
mailing it to himself, take a day or two to
get back to him, the theory being he might
pull some miracle out of the hat in those
few days, get himself some kind of grip.

Thinking of Jack now as I take one beer from
the fridge and place another from the cup-
board into the freezer, hoping the less I put
in all at once the less I'll take out in the
long run, the time it will take for them
to get cold etc., until the end of the night
that is, when I won't care anymore and I'll
drink them hot or cold, one after the other.

Jack disappeared one day, he was working
as the night councillor in a drug and alcohol
rehab, then he was gone, I heard back to
Arizona, homesickness or something,
or maybe not, no one was quite sure.

Hadn't thought of old Jack in a good long
while, then, like they say, all of a sudden
I could see him clear as day, his wiry frame,
his glasses and tight curly hair, the way he
stuttered when he came into the lounge beside
the offices that day, telling me it was none of
his business but man he thought I was making
a big mistake leaving rehab early, that really
the best thing I could do for myself was stay.

awake you want to start a dream but

you stretch and climb out
of bed. downstairs you stare
out the kitchen window. you
eat two strawberries. when
the neighbors come out of their
house you turn away. the cat
rubs against your leg. it might
be love but no, his bowl is empty,
all he wants is to remind you
of his needs. searching the night
and now morning you realize
you have slept nine hours. you're
tempted to go back to bed anyway,
maybe sleep three solid days
in a row. would that be such
a crime? instead you shower and
dress, put on shoes and a coat,
enter the slow turning
of participation, where minutes
fade into routine, and make
the hours disappear.

Watercolors

He told me I probably see the world differently
because I read and like art and write, claimed
it's likely I'm the same as his son-in-law because
his son-in-law paints. Maybe artists are like
black people: we all know one another and smoke
the same brand of cigarette. Maybe the son-in-law
stole his mother-in-law's panties like I stole a friend's
sister's panties out of their hamper when I was eleven
and took them home and kept them under my pillow
and pressed them to my face whenever I frenzied
my way through another session of jacking off.
I thought I was actually unique until I was seventeen
and realized most people have pissed in the shower
at least once. My mother used to tell her friends I was
strange. The first time I heard it I was twelve and
it hurt; those kinds of compliments kill when you're
insecure and adolescent. The crowd wants everyone
watching the same ticker tape; even if they don't
like you, to refuse to come out and play raises
the neighborhood's ire. Bukowski looked like a
janitor and punched like a truck driver mad at his
wife. He also gambled at the track like a thousand
dumb derelicts. Yeats' Irish tongue wove beauty
banged hard with truth. On a different page he bought
into the occult, too overwhelmed by his hard on to tell

Maud Gonn she was an idiot. The man who discusses
the price of a gallon of gas is not harming anyone
only losing himself in shitty minutia. Hopeless among
the line of dull days I used to spin myself dizzy with
powders that fog. High I claimed an edge, fancied myself
an adventurer, but it was all as common as bubbles
in a bath. Personally, I've known five suicides, including
the son-in-law that played with watercolors. They each
may have been at fault but it can be exhausting searching
the wide sky for wondrous roads, hoping for a Huck
Finn down the river with Jim on a homemade raft life.

The Making of a Writer

Broken by the age of ten, scared most
of the time but just didn't know it. That
curious belief everyone was better
at living than you. What ever would
make a person bury conversation
in their head, worried it would cost
the world if they made a mistake,
silence the tool to learn how stronger
mortals behave. So lonely young.
Then booze and drugs to buy peace.
Finally, out of the left corner
of nowhere, there's paper and pen,
and you begin writing one hail
Mary poem after another.

Speaking of Art

You grind the forks of the modified fork lift
into the air and though you can't see it clear
you attempt to pick the pallet of 140 6x6
posts off the beams. Oddly no one below bothers
to acknowledge death swinging over their
head. Bulling forward, unskilled you sweat
it to the ground somehow. Out on the back
lot you drop the awful load into a waiting
contractors banged to shit truck bed.
Punching out eight hours later it feels
evident the life you lead is murder.
Why didn't you ever bother to plot anything
out, put a world you might want into place?
All this redundant careening. For wasting years
God, if he exists, ought to resent each breath
he's allowed you to take. In the car home
the noise is no deity, only the radio playing
George Harrison's opening track on Revolver,
the quiet Beatle wailing about the taxman.
Speaking of art, you wrote a novel once.
It was about two people with battered pasts
in love living on the margins of New York
circa 1979. They had a good chance because
all they wanted was to survive. You lose hope,
they say, when you dream. Booze never

worked for you, drugs in the vein never
worked. Will the fork lift disappear
if you start a second book? Will the fear?
It all runs away the way Bukowski said,
like wild horses over the hills. Leaps
of faith land you in a haze, wondering.
Or like the sword in the neck of the bull,
they make you die. Either end anyhow
isn't going to hurt much, or at least for long

Angie

Angie says he'd rather pitch one inning for the Yankees, that he'd give up his three published collections of poetry, all he's ever written, in fact, for that single moment. You tell him he's full of shit, he stuffs more envelopes, does more readings than any other writer you know. He says you don't know any other writers except one. You admit it's true. Still, he stuffs a lot of envelopes; he's full of shit. Or maybe he's not. Who can understand another's dreams? Angie is sixty-three years old. He was never going to play major league ball, not even for the Texas Rangers, let alone the Bronx Bombers. Hell, he couldn't even play for the Mets. He takes vacation days to attend games, a bus and two subways to get to the House that Ruth Built. It's not the house that Ruth built anymore, just some conglomerates idea of a swank way to spend a sunny day. Ang is in the cheap seats rain or shine, ten or twelve times a year. You'd expect him in a bar weekends, rooting the old team on, boasting endlessly about his glory days on the mound for Archbishop Malloy, or some such school. It's not his style though, and thank Christ for that. You gave up on sports years ago so he sends emails talking instead about movies, books, music, writing. He has taste and has written two of the best poems probably ever written. His collection, One Fist Left In The Ocean

has more winners in it than the next hundred collections
you'll ever pick up, more than Wadsworth or Keats,
or William fucking Carlos Williams. Every interview
he gives, and yeah, he's a small press guy who actually
gets the opportunity to give interviews, if you can
believe it, he mentions America's pastime.
What the hell, Ang, you say, and he tells you again
about that wish to toss all he's ever written to the wind
for one pitch on the mound at Yankee stadium (that's right,
it's one pitch now) and you howl horse shit and he laughs.
Maybe he's pulling your leg. How do you write
the immortal (fuck you I'm not overstating it) lines
he has cut into paper and think like a sock hop loving
fifteen year old swathing linseed oil on his glove in his
room, discovering the oil is good lubricant for other
things before clicking the lock over, spreading
the kleenex out, dreaming of all those willing girls
a man might meet traveling with the team, a line
of beauties and half beauties no poet since Rumi has
ever encountered. Maybe he's not full of it after all.

Earth

The smell of it has always made
your head tilt upward with pleasure.
Men in hardhats moving dirt, the sight
of tree roots upturned, the widening hole.
It looked like a world to be in when
you were young, but you learned with
time it was drudge work, so many
crippled by the end of careers,
no pensions, no medical, their skills
their hands, their backs, which should
be enough, but never is. The whole thing
better at night anyway, with six drinks
in you, walking by in the dark, finding
your way around the plywood fence,
sitting with a moon only bright enough
for you. Stories in your brain then,
and song. Sadness everywhere,
and smiles. Memories always come,
bright ideas about some multitude
of futures, things that fade with first
light, but there is always that time,
before mortgages and troubled children,
before addictions and more life behind
than waiting ahead, dressed late afternoon
in fine clothing, waiting to leave for some
rare family celebration, eight or nine

years old, with a brother older by two
years. A mound of earth piled by the side
of what they were making into the new
telephone company. Skittish, knowing
it was trouble, but following that brother,
climbing, leaping, finally screaming
with joy, sliding on sharp pressed pairs
of trousers, the air cold with earth, hands
clenching dirt. Jimmy, who never worried
about curfews, or grades, never sweated
consequences, filthy with you that day,
on top of that mound when the old man
came around the corner yelling your names.
Fear all over your face, you still marveled
at the insolent shrug, the shit eating grin
on your crazy red headed brother's mug,
a man child ready, as ever, to do battle
with the one who'd long drank, and cursed,
and claimed some ham fisted hate
for his oldest, wild hearted boy.

No. 3 School

You don't remember her name. She
was nothing mean spirited or wild.
Kind maybe, it's impossible to tell, she
kept so much to herself in the grammar
school life you were all leading. Reddish
hair. Freckles. Breasts by the fifth grade.
For no reason at all, you targeted her,
days on end chasing her after classes,
a menacing fist held in the air, friends
laughing, egging you on as you followed
her down the street, all of you ducking
cars, full of adrenaline. This girl minding
her own business, dreading the last bell
because of you. One time she stopped
and turned. In a strained voice she flared
up at you asking, Why are you doing
this to me? Weakness, that's why, fear
of life, the need to make another feel
low to make yourself feel cool, a desire
to be liked by others in spite of the cost.
Though no apology matters, and how
could this make anyone feel better,
you've always wondered how long
it weighed on her, made her feel less
of a person, always hoped she's long
understood: none of it had anything
to do with who she was at all.

Big John

When John found trouble,
he joined the Navy, a ship
at sea, he was gone ten years.
I saw him yesterday, tall as
ever, back in his hometown,
crossing a parking lot, head
bowed, jangling change
in his pocket, bikers long
forgotten, that sour dope
deal that chased him away.
Big John, a church goer
now, married, three children
waiting in the car. With the
sun all across the lot, blazing
like any of a million mad
afternoons, he volunteered
about his unemployment,
house payments missed,
mouths to feed. Staring at the
horizon, shaking his head,
he turned finally to walk
away, hardly remembering
he used to know how to run

Broken

Tom on his bike, riding up and down the block, needing
a shave at fifteen, quiet and determined, squinting like he
didn't understand what you were saying, even when you
were just calling his name. Kids taunting him, tripping
him up with trick questions, watching his frustration grow
into anger, finally frightening them because they'd been
told retarded people didn't know their own strength, that
they'd squeeze the life out of you when they were only
trying to stop you from talking. This leafy neighborhood,
corner stores, chalk on sidewalks, dads commuting into
the city, home by five-thirty, dinner and the evening news.
Moms ironing clothes, cleaning dishes, watching soap
operas. Booze on New Year's, fireworks Fourth of July.
The Knights of Columbus sells raffle tickets. Memorial
Day there's a parade. One Spring Tom's bike is stolen.
He seems to decide the world is against him, stays
in doors two years. One woman in the neighborhood
hangs herself to get away from a gambling husband.
A blue haired matron living just down from the corner
continues to sing gorgeous melodies in church choir
while castrating her husband into a feeble man. Prom
season arrives, driver's licenses, part time jobs,
graduation. A girl who started drinking at ten throws
herself off a bridge. Tom, on a new bike, emerges,
telling everyone about his older brother going
to heaven after diving off a tree branch into a too

shallow pool of water. Bicycling the same old route,
he never bickers with his mother, stops talking to a sister.
Never lands a job, fails to keep his word. His children
are never born. No one from here can tell you more.
Only that one day he was gone again, like some
broken toy, he disappeared forever from the story.

When We Were Young

Kevin Gutt forgetting he had a soft heart,
trying to become a biker and failing on the
corner of 30th St. and Broadway. Cathy Lucas
and the Ruge girl, crashing bikes into the sides
of moving cars, crazy to see who could stop
themselves from falling. Little Eddie Fleet
in a pair of bell bottom jeans, with sparkle
covered platform shoes, high on acid in
Petey Boyle's backyard. The Padowsky
brother's grandfather spitting blood on his
stoop, drinking Schlitz beer in cans. A rope
swing under a half completed overpass,
leaping into sand and stagnant water,
bums there scavenging colored glass to
sell to mean tempered shop keepers on
Canal St. The priest who took your cousin
places like the Bronx Zoo because he
was a bad kid and his parents didn't know
what else to do with him. Christy Carter
pregnant, outside Ted's Deli, trying to
collect money to make it go away, turning
to wine, in fat gallon bottles, all afternoon
with Vinnie Marco, until her fourteen year
old legs could hardly walk straight, and
not a damn thing said at home to save her.

Crossroads

I was shooting hoops alone in the
schoolyard. He came up, a bottle
of water, shorts on, t-shirt. He was
a fat sweaty kid from the neighbor-
hood. Terrible stutter. Parents that
abandoned him, being raised
by a grandmother older than any
human the rest of us had ever seen.
Last name was Gutt, for a fat
kid a thing with its own set of grief.
He started running around the
court. After a couple of minutes
he gave up. After that I saw him
at it everyday for almost a week,
then no more. We all used to stutter
when he was around, call him
two-ton, fat boy. He made it look
like he didn't care. Gutt never
made the track team, the basketball
squad. I never saw him with a girl.
Later he dropped out of high school,
put on a dirty denim jacket,
a bandana. He started hanging out
on the corner, in front of Lucy's
bodega. One night I came up
the block and saw him there.

He stepped in front of me, started
growling, took a menacing stance,
got up in my face. I couldn't think
of anything to do but smile.
What's up Guttsy, how you been.
Another growl. Finally he backed
up, leaned against the bodega wall.
We talked a few minutes, mentioned
names of friends, forgotten times.
Later I heard he moved, that his
grandmother had died, that he'd
been stomped half to death in a bar
fight and quickly left town.

Gone

I'm thinking of that street I grew up on, the cement
and the few trees and the heat in summer like bricks
around a fire, winters with enough snow to pull a sled
down the middle of a dead avenue normally too busy
with traffic to cross without concern. Horns and sirens.
Telephone poles with rusted metal climbing spikes.
After a heavy rain we used to tie string around sticks
and fish garbage out of gutters, hang coat hangers down
sewers angling for Spaldeens or tennis balls. We played
running bases after supper until the street lights came on.
The houses were piled so close together you could hear
your neighbors argue, throw punches sometimes. Every
one smoked. Most people drank. My old man, he took
out whatever black hole was swallowing him on his wife
and kids, ranted, threatened, swore through vodka fumed
spittle he wished he'd never signed the adoption papers
making us his, said having children had ended his wine
and roses days. Beneath the terror I was still blue eyed,
thin as a rail, full of promise and dreams. A lot of years
stretched before me. I never bothered thinking about
time. Since then I've burned up whole decades,
neglected the writing I begged myself to do, forgot
about becoming an actor, forgot about bumming
around the world. Please, no new age meditation shit
about how we are always where we are supposed to be.
I never made a damn simple plan. Blew the one ride
allotted each of us so hard even a past I struggled to
survive has started looking like a good place to return.

Brother

Engine red hair
over smirks a thousand
yards wide, shrug
shouldered twelve
year old pot smoked
eyes took no care
or shit from anyone

across the city dump
trash piles of other
peoples lives the Hell's
Angels gave chase once
when you'd camped out
in that rust bucket thing
they claimed was their
abandoned van

hurrying over rats
over garbage roads
the bikers firing bb
rifles at your
hauling ass, your
two feet flying
for your life your
heart full of laughter

it was you that fished
for crabs, cages
dropped in greasy
hudson river waters
you that shoplifted
kite string, tied webs
across roads hoping
cars would hold

school all gone
by grade nine
eyes all hardened
favorite uncles
watch pawned
houses robbed
copper too off
telephone pole
wires

a weeping mother
threatened to turn
you in, dragged you
off to church instead
drunk father threatened
beatings, got you a job
at a friends umbrella
factory instead

thirty years gone
front tooth missing
hair long, you have
two ex-wives
three children high
as kites, a 12x15
apartment in an old
motel

it's you whose truck
won't start, cigarette
won't light, job won't
work, head too hard
mouth too certain, nails
all dirty, it's you with
a smile that shouldn't
be there, that won't fade

Shadows

My father came back to New York from New Orleans
raving about musicians on corners, bars with strange
lighting, carry out cups for your liquor, magicians,
jugglers performing. Somehow he didn't know all that
was available right down in the Village, a subway ride
away. Somehow he'd forgotten too that once he'd
wanted to be an artist, that there was a dust covered
box in the attic, his sketches, pen and ink, charcoal
drawings. In the 30's he was a child. His father beat
him and his brothers and mother regularly, drank
the family into misery. An uncle took pity, saw that
he had talent, talked of art college, of paying his way.
In the end a cousin with maybe a little more skill was
given the free ride. At twenty my father joined the
Navy. He landed in France at the end of the war,
came home, got a job in an honest to God insurance
company, married a solid woman, produced three
children, joined the Rotary Club, the Knights of
Columbus, drank himself silly on the same American
street as his old man, terrorizing his family too.
For forty years no one ever heard him talk about
the beauty of the sky, shadows marking trees,
the sound of tires on wet asphalt. He was never
caught daydreaming, reading, or going to museums.
Once, I showed him reams of poems I'd been

writing on loose leaf paper and he shook his head, marveling at how he hadn't known I'd been up to such things. One of us might have said more, started an actual conversation. Instead I can still see him sighing, reaching for the knob on the television set. He died at home at sixty-three from cigarettes and alcohol. I was almost a man by then. I thought I knew everything. I'd already been teaching myself for a long time to disregard him.

Dale

Poor Dale, always in the middle of worrying herself half to death, talking some daily
obsession over with saddened eyes, downturned mouth. The formality of a Tennessee
William's heroine, calling everyone, including her own mother, Mr. or Miss. *"Mr. Michael,
where were we?" "We weren't anywhere Dale. You just got here. What can I help you with."*
Really you can't help her with anything, she just wants to lay out some conjured dilemma,
some behavior she now wishes she hadn't gotten up to that morning because it made her
transport driver late and they couldn't stop to buy her scheduled cup of coffee The old girl.
Winters she wears a fake fur jacket that couldn't have looked good in the late seventies
when it probably was new. Hat to match. Giant purse stuffed with glitter shoes and Barbie
dolls. Stares at the phone wanting to call her case worker to question what time her doctor's appointment is a week
from tomorrow, though a calendar with her itinerary has been printed
and is gone over with her twice a day. *"Miss Cook? Aren't you forgetting something?"*
"What Dale. What am I forgetting." "Oh I don't know. Miss Cook? Where were we."

Nowhere Dale. Everything's fine. She takes out a snack, sits
   by herself. Asked to join
others she refuses. Prompted to work on a collage, she says
   no thank you, moves away
to another room. The staff call her sourpuss, laugh at her
   fretting, her insoluble problems.
"Oh Mr. Michael, what have I done. I can never go home now."
   "It's not time yet Dale.
You still have an hour before your ride." "I see. Well, it's all
   over now anyway."
No Dale. It'll be fine. Slow of foot, she retreats to the
   sensory room, closes the door
on herself, sits and screams, working out what can never be
   worked out. Returning
she says, "Mr. Michael, What's wrong with me?" "Nothing
   Dale. You're fine."
At a traffic light once, the center's van stopped next to
   Lorraine Carnelle, Dale's mother.
Miss Carnelle, Tammy, the driver, said, pressing her window
   down, "I have Dale
in the back, want to say hello?" "Not my day to talk to Dale,"
   the mother stated,
and drove away. Tammy told Dale her mother wanted her to
   know she loved her
very much. On a different day the van, riding over sleet
   covered roads, ended
up in a ditch. Dale repeatedly yelled from the back that she
   needed her coffee, were they

still stopping at McDonald's. Who can blame Tammy for
    wanting to hang her by her heels
out the window, let her Barbies and glitter fall like
    confetti. God love Dale. She dressed
in a wig and sparkly gown last Halloween, refused to respond
    to anyone who didn't
address her as Miss Gypsy, spoke all day in an otherworldly
    voice clearly not her own.
Darnell, mentally challenged, with advanced MS, choked on a
    pretzel once. Dale wouldn't
stop insisting something was wrong with Mr. Darnell until
    someone took action and saved
his life. Ask for a hug, Dale will lean in to you, press tight, a
    look of commiseration
implanted on her brow. Reach for her diet Coke she'll break
    your hand, move away
complaining the world is unfair, always trying to take another
    person's drink

Story

With each breath time thins
like a new mother. Bells
sound the years, brush our
arms. It all seems endless
while this second someone
has ceased to exist. New
leaves today. Sky gray blue
the horizon rounded.
At a window someone sets
a pair of reading glasses
on the bridge of their nose.
Spring becomes a Christmas
tree. The ocean waves.
You turn to tell a story
and are gone forever

You Turn Eighteen (Tucker Pavilion Adolescent Psychiatric Hospital)

Broken child your state of low
bangs hard inside me until I
feel dying is good art, or relief.
This spring day rises here as
nothing. The world's gifts lay
jagged, frozen. The mantra
in my head becomes, Let her
take what road she will, but
it is no answer, I can't release
myself from caring.

Child, I want to make you
crown yourself with edged
wonder, join the Peace Corps,
dig a well, smell green
pastures spread like Ireland
across a fogged dawn in some
mountain village. Leave
your bed sweet girl, shake
loose your history, the harm,
the sadness.

This fading late afternoon
watching you back from
some burnt outing I dance

in my head bright with love
until the pain of your
crippled crawling state
murders quick this
feted joy.

Child, my only child, born
this day years ago, I wish
you wonder, I wish you
splendor. True as wind the
scent of all in spite of wrong
that might be right coronates
the song. Suffering one why
in the name of things holy
is it you that cannot hear
such pleasure.

The Sound A Rattlesnake Makes

Leave by the front door, family already
gone getting groceries or new sewing
thread. Walk a great distance. By evening
catch a bus, a broken spring ride, exhaust
fumes through leaking windows, all the way
across the country. There, find a small
room in a town near the Mexican border.
Buy a new alarm clock. Hire on at the bar
downstairs. Sweep up, clear tables.
Once a month, cross into Mexico. Drink
whiskey, beer. Buy a whore, hopefully,
now and then, one that will at least pretend
to like Gringos. Slowly learn the patterns
of the sky, the sound a rattlesnake makes.
Never write home. Never return east. Late
one night, on a telephone at the end
of the hall, call drunk, tell your child you
are sorry, ask forgiveness, know, almost
before morning sobers you again,
you don't deserve it.

child

when I'm dead
she'll weep at
small moments,
remember little
idiosyncrasies
I was never aware
of. none of the
harder truths
will survive.
nostalgia,
newly born,
will change
me into a thing
worth clinging
to, shaping
an imperfect
man into
a dream

Today

Winter around the corner and your daughter's
best friend's father has been diagnosed with
leukemia. What miracle would see him live
another season remains unknown. Again you
think of the pain in your own back, all around
to the stomach, cramping whenever you sit,
how you keep meaning to quit booze, eat better,
exercise. Why you can't have pity for this
man lying in a cancer ward without bringing
yourself into it is beyond reason. Perhaps the
sky itself is to blame, the fact that heaven has
disappeared, and there are no saints on earth.
Tonight, before last light, you look at the
leaves covering the lawn, see the wind rattle
them, hear that sound. With the moon hard in
the east a dog erupts down the street, a car
starts in a neighbors driveway, a child yells
for a playmate to hurry. One hundred years
from this moment, nothing anyone has done
today will be remembered. Let us pray.

Funeral

Ten days ago my mother took her last breath. Too weak, too
    old, she gave
way in a hospital bed after eighty-five years on earth, calling
    for her dead
sister, her dead mother, chasing after them maybe, having
    believed all her
life in God, heaven, the church, Saint Peter, Rome. Whenever
    she felt taken
for granted she'd tell my brother and sister and I we'd miss
    her when she was
gone. We had nothing in common really, hardly spoke these
    last years. I'll
tell you though, as a kid Little League game day meant the
    world to me. On
the field, taking my swings, on the mound, my arm against
    the batter. When
summer would break nasty with a heavy thunderstorm I'd
    beg my mother
to drive down to my game, tell her maybe it would let up, if it
    stopped we'd
play. The sky dark as midnight, rain relentless, knowing it
    wasn't going to
stop anytime soon, she got in the car every time. Sighing,
    driving, she'd circle
the small parking lot, point out the empty field, no coaches,
    umpires, security

gate locked across the refreshment stand. Giving in I'd agree
   to leave. Hair
getting soaked, clothes getting wet, we'd run to the house
   through the storm.

At the wake those rains, that ball field, her housecoat, her
   short, close cut
hair not yet gray come back to me clear as if it were all
   happening right
then. From a million miles away the sweet smell of a leather
   baseball mitt
chokes me with tears. My daughter, my only child, puts her
   seventeen
year old arm through mine. This girl, always reticent, her
   emotions mostly
held tight inside, is suffering a lonely, crushing adolescence,
   but she takes care
of me now, whispering she loves me, squeezing tighter
   through my suit jacket.
Friends from when I was a kid come up to the coffin. I
   haven't been within
three states of any of them in twenty-five years. With what
   time has done
I don't recognize one of them. He laughs when finally I do,
   says, Hell, we've
only known each other since we were two. But we don't know
   each other.
We never did. We never will. My own daughter often makes
   me confused.

I can't understand why she lives the same mistakes I did. I've
    warned her,
schooled her. But I am a fool. She's choosing her own life. It
    doesn't matter
what my road has been, how much I want to make every
    minute of hers better.

It's been twenty-five years since my father died. He used to
    come home drunk,
angry, drag us out of bed with his miserable voice,
    threatening, a fist at his
wife's face, spitting out how useless we were, that he never
    wanted us.
My mother made it my job to corral him into bed. Once
    when I was ten she
became infuriated with me when I failed to pull the blinds
    down while
undressing him. When we gave her lip about anything she'd
    threaten us,
tell us she'd kick us where it hurt. My brother cries for the
    first time
in his life that I've seen, leaning a hand on my mother's coffin.
    His anger
has always seemed to come in bursts of strange tales. At fifty-
    three he still
claims to admire biker gangs, stumblebum thieves. He had it
    harder than
my sister and I. Anyone might say with his wild streak and
    disdain for truth
he brought it on himself. But after all, *he* was the child when
    it began.

Standing in this suit I haven't worn in years lights flicker
outside the visitation
room, the funeral parlors way of signaling mourners it's time
to say your
final goodbyes. In my life I've been so angry with my child
I've wanted
to throw her through a wall. It may be a particular kind of
sadness
that I claim it as an achievement that I've never done it, that
she's never
even heard me say I want to. Seeing my daughter staring at
him one of my
old friends calls across the viewing room: We look like old
men, he says,
but we're still only eight years old. He's half dumb, and has
always been
ridiculous, but there's truth in that. I weep once more,
turning back,
catching the funeral director closing the coffin lid. My
mother will never
walk across a room again, smile the way she always did,
embracing
people. I love my daughter's head resting then on my arm,
her silent
sign of comfort and love. I miss my mother, like she said I
would.

Replenishment

The trees stand in the rain, full of movement.
The clouded sky lets loose with the sound
of replenishment, the sidewalks dark with it.
Time remains strictly a concept. In spite of that
I feel further behind places I want to be, sense
the end of roads I'll be allowed to know. Still
I remember the strident wonder built into
the smell of an oiled baseball mitt, the glove
taken from a box in a closet when spring arrives.
With luck I'll wake into morning. The world will
unfold all over me as I try for everything again.

A Simple Thing

I picture her in a bathing
suit at a pool on Sixteenth
St. I picture a Buick le
Sabre, we're holding hands
in the front seat. I picture
her with a beer in a bar,
an Irish band playing
on a small stage. I
picture that afternoon
in my parents living
room, she was standing
there with a pair of
panty hose on and not
much else. I picture
the phone ringing, her
voice, a simple thing.
I picture the Thanks-
giving day football
game, the big game,
that year in her white
Micheline tire man coat.
I picture her young, and
myself young too, back
when everything was
possible and impossible

at the same time, the
air we breathed, the
rush of new things,
so alive then it hurt
just to walk across a
room. Those days be-
fore knowledge settled
things, when the world
could still break your
heart like thunder

Everything

October rain has stopped and
cars are pressing spray from
wet streets. A man with large
hands, drunk, stops, talks to
you, walks away. A girl then,
turns a corner, smiles shyly,
waves slightly, her blue eyes
breathing I'm cold into your
ear. Your arms fold around
her, warm her with all of you.
Falling back together your
two bodies find the wall of
a store, everything closed
on the street but your lives,
one night years ago, when
you were still young and
knew everything would
always be this way

About Fourteen Years Old

An empty schoolyard, early
evening, the hard air of
October, I'm alone near the
basketball courts, I cross
the blacktop in my converse
high tops, in my army style
jacket, hands buried in
the jacket's pockets, it's
Bayonne, New Jersey and
probably I'm fantasizing
about a train ride to Georgia,
or a girl with long brown
hair, I take a hand from my
pocket and run it along the
brick wall of the school, I
come to the chain link fence
surrounding the schoolyard
and run my hand along that
too, the traffic light on the
corner changes, the cars begin
to move again, the fall sky
slate gray, getting darker by
the minute, tumbling by

Trick or Treat

They came thru the cold, over crackling leaves, wearing
their costumes, holding out their bags, their pillow cases.
You dropped the candy in, smiled, told them how good,
how scary they looked. For two hours they were all over
the neighborhood, running, laughing. Finally it slowed to
a trickle, a few stragglers hurrying before it was too late
and their parents said enough. Then, when the door bell
hadn't rung for maybe half an hour, he came along. Tall
and lean, hair cropped short, wearing a blue t-shirt and
black pants, the pants an inch too short, no socks or coat,
a scuffed pair of wing tip dress shoes on his feet. You
recognized him of course, he lived only a few blocks
away, with his parents and brother and two sisters, in
a two room cold water flat above Whitey and Lefties bar,
on 28 th St. He was around fifteen, sixteen, old enough
that the neighbors talked about it the next day, clucked
their tongues and laughed. Five months went by before
you thought of him again. It was an article in the paper.
Reading it, you remembered him hurrying from house
to house that night, almost running, how he said
thank you when, not wanting to give him the good
stuff because he was too fucking old and ought to
know better, you dropped a handful of rock hard
bazooka bubble gum into his brown paper bag,
remembered every inch of him as you looked at
the accompanying photographs, his two younger

sisters, age six and four, being taken out of the home by protective services, parent's charged with child neglect, pile of empty beer cases under the sink, no food in the opened fridge, no electricity, no bedding on the mattresses, a frightened dog, bone thin and sad eyed, standing in a corner

Poem Written Upon My Daughters Graduation From Elementary School

She could be an actress on
Broadway, land in the field
of molecular biology, search
out cures for terrible diseases.
Maybe she will work as a
stringer for a newspaper, file
stories from war zones. Maybe
she will photograph polar ice
caps on the bering sea. She will
not settle in this place, love here,
marry here, have two children,
two cats, a dog, a two story
house with a garage. She
will not join the P.T.A, or bake
brownies for Cub Scouts. She
must burn harder than that,
love much, lose much, fall
through a great city on her
knees, make great things
out of fear, out of longing.
She must find her work and
treat it like prayer, chase
one thing she cannot help
but cherish. Darling, open
the world and drink from it,
or you will break my heart

It Wasn't An Unusual Night

You driving. Both of us eighteen, nineteen years old.
We pull into a gas station. There, at the other pump,
the almost famous band from our little enclave of blue
collar Jersey, the rockers, Moonbeam. What was it,
1981? We'd been searching for weed, and we ask
the half Spanish, half black lead guitarist with
the Chinese eyes if they might have some to sell.
He laughs. We got some, he drawls. We're only
looking for a nickel bag. He takes the five spot
and hands us a small manila envelope stuffed full.
Enjoy, he says, laughing again. There's so much
of it we wonder if we've been beat. Ten minutes
later Mark is doing five miles an hour
on the Boulevard and I'm telling him slow
down man, slow down, him wondering
if I'm right, are we going to crash? Zonked,
we head to a guy's place whose name I've forgotten.
He lived above the bar his old man owned.
His parent's were gone somewhere and there'd
been a party. It was three or four in the morning
by now; what was left of the crowd had crashed
on floors, couches. Mark tells the guy he ought
to go downstairs, open the bar. Instead we smoke
a little more and pass out. An hour or two later,
Mark starts yelling fire, fire. Everyone in a stupor
rolls to their feet, frightened. Mark's laughing,

cracking himself up. We leave then for bacon
and eggs at the shitty Greek diner a few blocks away.
What the fuck kind of shit was in that weed? Mark
asks. I blink and laugh. Jesus Christ, I say, fucking
Moonbeam. When I'm dropped off at my house
we somehow miss the hearse that's already there,
parked at the curb, close to the telephone pole.
Inside I find them zipping closed the black bag.
Something is said to me but I don't remember what.
I know soon enough: the booze and cigarettes have
finally choked my father's heart too hard. I'll never
forget stupidly wondering how in the world anyone
might breathe, shut off in a bag that way. I'll never
forget the years it took to stop feeling bad that I'd been
out living another idiot night while my old man died,
on the sofa, in his sleep. In the morning my mother
and sister and brother together, sitting with the body
after he was gone, waiting for the right people
to arrive, to clean away the horror fresh death is.

Crazy

We're drinking beer, in his garage. Pointing out past the open garage door, he explains the neighborhood: this one's that, that one's this; not like where we grew up, he says, no one knows anyone here, they keep to themselves, not friendly at all. Draining the end of a can, he lights a cigarette, nods, grins. You remember, he says, up at the high school, that turkey we stole? Cooked and stuffed and everything. The things we did, he laughs. Remember Jen? She was wild, that one, my first love. Those were the days, huh. He grabs two more beer and we sit in the folding chairs on either side of the cooler. The summer air hovers over the cement. A dry breeze rustles the trees. He tells a story of a car accident, a late night when we were teenagers, coming from a bar, how the car flipped and we walked away without a scratch. He tells me no one was like us, that we were crazier than anyone. I wipe my brow, try to smile. From the corner of the house, his young son and daughter appear. They turn on the hose, start spraying water toward the open windows

of the minivan in the driveway. His wife
yells from the kitchen about the burgers
we've forgotten turning black on the grill.
I think, just briefly, of a picture I once saw
of my old man when he was maybe forty,
standing with a drink, in plaid shorts, next
to a picnic table in some backyard, sunlight
reflecting off his glasses. I remember
how old I'd once thought he'd been then,
how younger he was than I could have
imagined. Putting my can of beer down,
squinting into the light of the bright day,
I realize I have a headache, that I wish
I was home, reading a book, in the living
room, with my wife and daughter.

Mental

The road to pick up Marty, a client
in the support center for the mentally
challenged where you work, runs
through the countryside. You take
the trip every morning about six-
thirty. Black as night in winter.
Sun just rising summers. Nothing
but blacktop, trees, chicken farms
a mile off the road. Sometimes you
wonder if you actually sleep through
part of the drive. This morning
the radio is loud though, a half lame
shock jock cracking jokes about butt
cracks and anal sex, and you think some
more about that girl from your youth,
the one in your dream the night before.
She was all filled out, curvy in the
netherworld, half pretty half odd looking
in some strange sexy way. There's miles
of grassland out the windshield, short
trees that look like sagebrush. There's
a little pull off circular road, a neat
trimmed decorative sign stating it was
Robert E. Lee's last camp ground before
surrendering at Appomattox. The radio

host's sidekick sounds like a wet dream.
Her name is Diane too, same as the old
neighborhood girl lingering in your head.
Tires on gravel, engine in park. It's
amazing how quick a man can masturbate,
even so close to Lee's final shame.
Pressing a window down when done
you hear an owl, the last of it probably
before it sleeps. You recall all the times
you spotted county sheriff's cruising these
switchback roads. Spilling water from
a Deer Park bottle you clean your hand.
Car back in drive you hit the radio button.
Bowie sings *ch-ch-changes. Don't tell
them to grow up and out of it,* he pleads.
Grimacing or grinning, you don't know
which, you think of Marty, quiet Marty
holding his head, rocking, anxious about
unknown fears. And the sunlight gets
full and white in the sky. And the day
is gonna' be heavy soon with the mental
boys and girls calling your name.

Support Specialists For Mentally Challenged Adults

Stacey drinks nights, comes in still loaded,
pops some pills and gets worse as the day goes
on. Tammy stirs the pot, sidles up to co-workers,
makes wicked comments, complains, says
it's all ridiculous, the way the place is run.
Amy wants a promotion. She says there needs
to be a floor supervisor for when the program
manager is away, states she's brought this up
countless times, that Michelle knows it's true
but hasn't done a thing about it. She calls over
to Michelle's office four or five times a day,
makes full reports, feeds into the delusion
that we can change the clients we have, make
them somehow different than they are, plays
coy, building an alliance with the boss, gunning
for a job that doesn't exist, never helping
others while everyone else does. The new
guy Daryl seems to have his hands on clients
too much, touching, tickling, I don't know
yet, you might say groping. He laughs about
everything, agrees about everything, says yes
when you ask if he's toileted so and so though
you never see him in a bathroom. Someone
quits about every month. College kids
do a summer, promise to return during winter

break, never do. We wipe asses, take punches,
break up fights, perform the Heimlich, administer
anti-psychotic meds, listen to our names called
a thousand times a day by the neediest people
the world has yet to create, loving some, hating
others, joking no matter what day it is at least
there's always a Friday, closing the door
in the restroom, turning on the sink, screaming
silently into the mirror for ten bucks an hour.

Nothing

Behind the wheel, he was talking about
killing a bookie, he owed the guy so much
money. He was laughing, not wanting really
to kill anyone, then the car flipped, the two
of them upside down, sliding thirty, forty
feet. A black Trans-Am, classic muscle car
of that era, all smashed to hell on Route 440.
Both of them were eighteen, twenty, drunk,
four-thirty in the morning. Soon enough
there were sirens, cops, an ambulance.
My friend, the driver, walked away with
scratches. The other one was banged up bad,
leg busted, nose splattered across his face.
For years afterward they'd run into each other
in one bar or another, my guy always wishing
to avoid the other, whose nose had been fixed
in a not great way, whose voice, since the accident,
stayed a nasal twang out of some movie maybe
about a half wit who tried too hard. They'd
shake hands. My friend would apologize.
The other guy would smile. Sounding like
a mosquito buzzing an ear, he'd say, it's nothing,
it all worked out okay. The two of us would
leave quick then, on to another dive bar
in the Chevy, Nova that had replaced the Trans,
roaring away in the dark, my boy, all of a sudden

angry, saying he couldn't take running into the guy,
that he was a jerk, talked too much, married
a slob, why the fuck is he always out anyways,
he'd ask, his voice smooth as a whisper, his nose
a Roman copy of Brando's, circa Tennessee
William's A Streetcar Named Desire.

911

You pick up the straw, snort a quick thin line of
coke, do another, then another. You pour whiskey
over ice, sip it. You have four bags of heroin. When
the coke races your heart, sweat staggering from
your temples down the sides of your face, you
tap a little of the H out to calm things down. The
refrigerator sounds that strange buzzing noise, the
lights flicker on the tv. How many hours go by,
you'll never know. Somewhere late in the night,
you relax a bit too much, feel your heart rate slow,
your blood pressure drop. You think if you close
your eyes too long, the last breath you'll ever take
will ease from your mouth and go away. Fighting
it, you walk from the couch to the front door.
Finding the cold steel of the door, you press your
forehead against it. Your eyes tremble, float back
up inside your head. It scares the hell out of
you and you pick up the phone finally and dial
911. You tell the operator you're having trouble.
She wants to know what the trouble is. While she
talks, you open the front door, step out onto the
stoop. You take a breath of air, then another.
Somehow, things begin to feel ordinary again,
as if the emptying of your life has subsided.
The operator wants to know if she should send
an ambulance. You tell her no, you think you'll

be all right. Sir. Are you sure? I'm sure, yes, I
think I am. Sir? No. I'm certain operator, thank
you. After you hang up, you begin to worry they
will send a patrol car to check on you anyway.
Carefully, you push the dope and the straw
and the razor blade you were cutting the stuff
with to the center of the mirror. You place
the mirror in the cabinet below the sink in the
bathroom. Back on the couch, you listen for
sirens, stare at the front door knob. After ten
minutes, you take the mirror back out, put it
back on the table in front of the couch, cut
a little coke from the pile, pick up the straw

Falling

In Harlem, on 119th St., the 3rd floor of a depleted brownstone, they sold the stuff in the back apartment. After you got what you wanted you could go into the front room and shoot up. There were always stained cartons of Chinese take-out on the floor, discarded bottles, empty matchbooks. There was a cot pressed against one wall, a mess of sheets bunched somewhere near the foot of it. There was an old brown couch too, and a folding chair with one leg dented almost in half. It was hard to balance on the chair but if you really wanted to you could make it work. When all the seats were taken, I'd push garbage out of the way and sit on the floor. I'd stare at nothing, dope running thru my veins, wondering if I was going to puke. Most of the time no one said much. Sometimes the dealers would set up sticks of incense, they'd light them so you'd almost not smell the sweet, sour odor of sweaty sick people. Sometimes I'd think about when I was a kid, remember stickball and fire escapes and rooftops, punch ball and drinking soda and laughing hard enough

that the soda came thru your nose. I'd
remember running bases and summer,
those warm clean days when we had
nothing to do, how we'd toss rocks thru
branches of trees, pick up sticks and
break them over our knees, try and write
a message on the sidewalk with the
sharpened tips of them, how we'd ride
our bikes fast, happy with the breeze, and
the sun, riding no hands, with our eyes
closed, hardly worrying about falling

August

You can't help thinking of being a kid, caught in summer
   storms,
trying to dodge rain drops, running fast until your breath
   deserted
you, pulse pounding in the temples. All concrete then,
   buildings
on top of one another, backyards the size of manhole covers.
Everyone spent a lot of time looking at cracks in the sidewalk,
talking about digging holes to China, climbing telephone
   poles.
On rooftops we walked one leg in the air on ledges, playing
ball in traffic we moved only as many inches as it took not to
get hit by passing Chevrolets, dumb as cigarette smoke
   because
death wasn't real in our hearts yet. Along the way some of us
started pitching no hitters in little league, hitting twelve,
   fifteen
long balls in a season of eight or ten games. High school then,
all-county maybe, never all-state, never the majors, never
a college like Auburn, Texas A&M, places where the cleats
were cleaned by clubhouse managers and the balls were
whiter than Christmas. Always back to blue collar worlds,
to work in insurance, join the fire department, the police
   force,

build pensions, families. Eventually a move to the suburbs,
where you drink too much, smoke too much, remember
the old playing field, the twelve year old championship game
when younger kids ran to the outfield fence when you were
up, waiting for the home run ball they could return for a ticket
for a free popsicle at the concession stand, some neighborhood
mom sweaty there, yelling not to run near the stand with
so many people around, sit Saturday afternoons watching
Yankee games on WPIX, knowing you'd never been good
enough, quietly wondering anyway if maybe you had.

Listen

The clear day changed as you watched
the green trees in summer heat. Black clouds
covered the sun, rain came hard, banging
the earth, houses, everything. Within minutes
the world soaked, the sun back, a thick branch
down in the yard, debris everywhere like war
torn Europe. Screened windows let a taste
like childhood in. This small roar through
a slow afternoon called you to it but like a lot
of things you failed to listen, missing the wet
on your face, the wind around your body,
a flood like tears, lethargic in a chair in a room
that will always be less everything

Other World

You strip down, put on your
suit. In the backyard you walk
to the white steps, fall into the
water. The lights of the pool
splash on the trees, the moon
gray blue thru the branches.
You wallow around, dive to
the bottom, stay down as
long as you feel you can.
The water, stirred, slaps
against the stone coping.
There's the sound of a
screech owl overhead,
cicadas clacking, crickets.
On your back, floating, you
think, where are the bricks,
the pavement, sirens, car
horns, radios, shouts from
corners, the human voice in
full vibrato. Bloated in the
warm night, muted like a
mule that has lost its kick,
you wonder if in your life
you'll ever have a full
bright, heart popping

moment again, or even
just a decent pastrami on
rye, daily news in your lap,
cold beer in a mug, after
midnight, some Tuesday
night, lower eastside,
New York, at a crowded
table in Katz's deli

Eying The Clock

The drive to work should be a meditation,
Ben Webster maybe, or Stan Getz
hitting long slow notes.

There's not much traffic going in,
trees and cows after the highway, dark
out six thirty in the October morning,
alone behind the wheel.

You end up anxious anyway, pushing,
trying to get morning tea at Murphy's before
a certain time, rushing to hit the side road
so you can park and eat the horribly thick
honeybun you swear never to buy again
and always do.

Pushing pushing pushing.

Eying the clock on the dash, hurrying to save
time to sit, watch, breathe.

Parking, you piss next to a tree.

Three horses really come to life in the pasture
across the road, through the mist the utter cliche
of majestic, alive in real time.

Tapping the wheel, you wonder, is it early
enough to stay? Will you be late if you wait?

Last week you picked up *Essential Teachings,*
by the Dalai Lama.

The Dalai Lama has to be able to help calm
this roaring, rushing nothing in you, there since
you were eight years old, existing for no reason
you have ever been able to find.

On the first page His Holiness talks about there being
no I, and you stop reading because all you know
is I.

The Dalai Lama must have a good life.

Then again

At home in his monastery the other monks
must duck away so they are not seen when
he passes by.

Better to do the ducking away, you think.

Writing this poem you lose concentration
planning what movie you should watch
when you are done.

Tomorrow you might try Dinah Washington
singing smoky forties tunes.

Maybe that will work.

Taboo

Last night you dreamt about work again.
Staff and clients were all dead. The afterlife
was an abandoned factory, smashed springs
and glass all over the floors. We all walked
around in our death clothes, doing what we'd
done when we were alive, trying to understand
when we might be allowed to rest. The dream
ended with silence, with wind banging shutters
that made no noise, the old broken apart factory
empty again. Yesterday on the job Stephan
cursed you and you cursed back. He's mentally
challenged. You're supposed to guide him into
learning better social skills. His anger kept
escalating. So did yours. Late in the afternoon,
he punched a co-worker in the face. At home
you sat on your couch searching your own
behavior. Might be you're more like him
than seems possible. Always you've suffered
the ridiculous taboo, that violent machismo
is manhood. You reject it but revert to it
constantly, failing through the years to control
it with Buddha, or Christ, or booze or drugs.
Before you left for the day a happier client,
Danny, sang Irish songs, his voice loud,
off key. He reached in his pocket when you
stood with him, handed you your glasses.

I picked these up off the floor after Stephan
knocked Shannon in the head and you all fell
over the big chair, he tells you. You took
the glasses and hugged him. He wanted
to know if you were okay. I'm okay Danny,
thanks. You like the Irish on my phone Mike?
You like the Irish on his phone plenty. And his
beautiful crooked grin. And his abandon belting
out music. And you know you gotta' leave
this gig before it kills you, or you kill someone.

Danny

Sometimes they take him off the van in the morning
and it's like a convicted murderer being hustled down
the row toward the death chamber, three or four people
around him, hands at his elbows, ushering him along
on his crippled legs, keeping him from assaulting staff
or peers, getting him to a bench in front of the care
facility, telling him all the way that it will be all right,
sitting with him there, asking what's wrong, knowing
the most he can ever come up with is that he's frustrated,
a word he's been taught to use when he has no words
for whatever brain malady at birth made him unable ever
to choose his own dinner, understand the premise of the
simplest children's movie, go on a date with a person
he might one day love. With his balding head. With his
neatly trimmed mustache. The cellphone he loves blares
bad Christmas music beginning in July. He's a man child
with a grip stronger than a fleet of destroyers at sea.
He grabbed a workers hair between his fingers once,
pulled her low. He was about to start raining blows
on her head but was stopped just in time. That same day
he sang like always, off key, loud with joy. When asked
if he thought he had a good voice he replied without
hesitation, No. Then he began the song all over again.
Listen Michael, he said, *I'm singing fiance,* meaning
Beyonce. Holding his poor deformed hand aloft
he shakes it along to the music, a grin wide enough
to beat the world all over his forty-three year old face.

When a game show comes on in the tv room and a buzzer
sounds he tells the television to stop farting. He thinks
the word beer is funny. And the word poop. The bastard
has charisma. All the other clients who aren't afraid
of him love him to death. There are parents still alive
who love him. Two brothers who love him, two sisters.
Still, he's in a group home. It was overwhelming
for his mom and dad. As they aged the demands
on their time, the acting out. Physically he'd started
to hurt them. What care worker has ever loved a person
the way a parent does? How many swings with his fist
before Danny's shoved against a wall, his head pressed
into the sheetrock? Unless they die first and early a home
is pretty much where every mentally challenged adult
in America ends up. Ten dollar an hour people with maybe
two jobs and not enough sleep paying rent on a place
a lot less nice than where their charges live. A lot
of the world is as angry as Danny sometimes is. All
bruises aren't raised by accident. Thursday of the week
just gone by Danny apologized to me when I was putting
him in the car for an outing in the community. The seatbelt
wouldn't click closed. *Jesus*, I'd said, *this belt is bizarre*.
His voice in response was high and sad and desperate.
It was all up to me whether he got to go on that ride;
he didn't want my mood or problems to get in the way.
It was beautiful and honest anyhow, the words he
spoke: *I'm sorry the seatbelt's bizarre Michael*.

Danny, Again

Larry died. He'd been going to the center
for mentally disabled adults where I work
for almost ten years. He was a decent man
of sixty, always thirsty from the meds
he had to take, willing to steal any drink
left alone for even a single moment, but
in all, a kind, non verbal gentleman, never
really bothering anyone. All day Larry
walked back and forth through our rooms,
anxious, smiling, sitting now and then,
but never social with his peers. We went
as a group to the funeral, escorted a few
clients, said goodbye in our way, not
knowing any of Larry's elderly relatives.
Days later, Danny, one of our most
talkative guys, needy as hell, full of life,
always grabbing for attention, wanting
an audience, was by himself in the small
front room, seated on the ratty couch
in there, clueless that I'd come up,
that I was standing outside the door.
With some bit of formality, he cleared
his throat, tuned his always present phone
to the song, Amazing Grace, announced,
This is for you Larry, then, in his horribly

off key voice, sang along full throttled,
stating afterward, We love you Larry,
we miss you, months later still the only
person to mention Larry Taylor's name,
the single voice remembering, since they
put that quiet, lonely soul in the ground.

Locked Unit Psych Ward Cornel Medical Center New York City

David mans the bank of public phones across from the nurses
    station.
He answers calls and calls out patients names whose loved
    ones dial in.
He's friends with everyone, giving advice, shaking hands,
    shouting
I'm strong, see, raising arms in muscle poses. Sixty year old
    Hasidic
Jew, manic as a mission to the moon, we call him the mayor
    and hug
goodbye each night, virtual strangers three days ago, he's easy
    to like,
which is hard to be when you talk twenty hours a day non
    stop.
Gerta steals empty plastic cups and food wrappers and forks,
hoards it all in her room, screams unbridled hate at the
    attending
doctor then seconds later thanks him profusely for answering
a question, telling him he's kind, wonderful. She waits each
    night
in a chair facing the east river to watch the tugboats come by
at six-fifteen, telling all who might listen it's what she's in here
    for.
Lena is overweight but thinks she's starving to death. Any
    food

brought from outside by any visitor she makes a B line for,
staring angrily, like a child, asking, Can I have some? Henry
paces circles back to front across the floors. When asked
   about
his family he says he was raised by animals. My sister took
   my
manhood, he shouts one day, then asks for some special hat
he brought in with him. Denied this privilege he returns
to walking, skinny arms swinging hatefully. Poor Robert,
still baby faced at nineteen, he has both hands bandaged
from fingertips to wrists; He climbed through a panel
in the bathroom ceiling, tried to claw his way past sheet
metal into the ducts, as if he were living some mental ward
movie, as if he might actually have been able to find his way
free. New arrival stumbles shell shocked, his pants falling
toward his ankles every few steps, no underwear he makes
an impression, raising cackles of complaint from half
the unit, until they put him in hospital gowns, one around
   his
front, one tied in back. He bellows when he drinks his
   kindergarten
sized carton of milk, hides the television remote so no one
else can use it. Twenty-nine year old Amanda's father
visits, giving back rubs to his near psychotic grown child,
rubbing eskimo kisses with her until word spreads he must
be molesting her. Staff here circle, three to every patient.
They make notes, take head counts, yawn and nod
   ambivalently

at every lunatic request. Three locked doors to the elevator.
Visiting hours eleven a.m. to seven p.m., seven days a week.
We stay for all of them, ten days straight, never after the first
hours ever finding the heart to say why our quiet kind
   eighteen
year old blue eyed child has ended up in such a place.

Mea Culpa Mea Maxima Culpa

It's getting dark outside the kitchen window forty years ago.
The air is probably crisp, the month, I'm certain, October.
The waiting may have been the worst part of it then.
By five-twenty, if the car hadn't pulled into the driveway
everything was likely to go haywire. Foolish to wait
on the front porch with fingers crossed but until you were
a teenager it's what you did. All that worry never changed
an outcome. Don't think anymore he meant to be that way.
Booze and furor. So much anger. Anyone might think a person
would give up the rye and vodka, knowing it turned their
every thought ugly, every action violent. How often does
change occur in people though. Today finds you with
a litany of your own mistakes, wounding a child of your
own, failing a wife who only ever tries to be kind.
Once you asked your mother why she didn't leave him.
Where would I go, she wanted to know. But she loved him,
it's clear having heard the things she said after he was dead,
how it had been early for them, before you were born.
Love can remain inexplicable to any outsider, even
the children of those who seemed torn apart, those who
were welded together by a marriage full of everything.

The Alarm Rings

Five thirty in the morning. The alarm rings, I reach
for the button and instantly my thoughts are dark.
Moments that appear bright end as quick as they start.
The child I love is falling apart. I could weep, plain
and simple, but what has that ever done. I could give
in to angry outbursts too, but contributing bad feelings
to another's troubles is an awful game. This is all burnt
hours and pain. When I was small I waited nights for
a father to come home hoping he'd be sober. I wanted
to avoid hours of ugly fighting. My fears, my worries
then, they never prevented a thing. I grew old enough
to be gone, that's all, old enough for him to become
a memory. In middle age my stomach folds in on itself
again. Staring out windows I anticipate car headlights,
arrivals. Children live their own lives, destroy themselves
if they wish. It's hardly a comfort thinking you can
help, learning your pleas, your sense, your direction
will always be discarded. It's horrible knowing someone
wants to die, horrible loving them more than you love
yourself. I think of the scent of moved earth, I'm nine
or ten, peering through a hole in a plywood fence at an
excavation site. Chestnuts cut in the center to make rings,
garage roofs tar paper soft with Converse high tops
running, jumping from one wobbly landing to another.
On a Schwinn bike with sissy bars and plastic handle

grips, riding between red faced Kiwanis Club members parade day 4th of July weekend, all the time in the world in my levi jeans, heart full of hero worship for the Bronx bombers gruff number fifteen, his new pilot's license and plane crash waiting in Ohio, the summer of '79, playing hard in the dirt in the house that Ruth built.

Words

You think it's easy for a minute then it gets
painfully hard again. Days of cold skies
that ought to be prettier, rolling black thunder
of summer storms beautiful, your mind too
steady to break, so it cracks. Oh you want
to sing and smile, you want to cry. Someone
closer to you than your own breath is hurting,
perpetually. Heavy with the afternoon, you take
milk from the fridge, sit with a newspaper,
scan with little interest what others call tragedy.
And this guy too, who you grew up with,
a man you haven't seen in thirty years,
who always seemed humble, caring, has had
a stroke. They discovered a cancerous tumor,
in his head. You're in touch on Facebook.
You tell him you're hoping for an upswing
for him, what with the radiation over now.
He replies, Yeah, me too, highlighting
the uselessness of your words, all words,
though you have been most touched in life
by words, in books, in music, once or twice
from people alive in a room even. Sweet child,
I love you. Your laugh is the universe.
Bury fast the past, it is done. Find a way back
to what you might be. I don't give a damn
what you think is paradise, just make it
earthbound, alive. Make it sun and wind,
hug it until it grows, show me with your
terrible, wonderful smile.

Michael Flanagan was born in the Bronx, N.Y. and raised in the New York Metropolitan area. He currently resides in Richmond, VA, but is planning a move away from there in the very near future. He can be reached by email at: michaelflan44@gmail.com

www.ingramcontent.com/pod-product-compliance
Lightning Source LLC
Chambersburg PA
CBHW030120100526
44591CB00009B/469